My Last Words To You

ISBN: 979-86-533-0088-2

To you, the one who bought this book and is going to read it, I hope you enjoy it.
It might be just another book you're buying, but it means the world to me and motivates me to keep writing.
I hope you'll heal from things you don't talk about, whether it's a broken heart, family problems or something else.
That you'll learn to love yourself and put yourself first.

I also would like to thank my family, friends and my editors E-ditto.

Lots of love
Lamara Djabraïlova

Lamara Djabraïlova

after weeks of not seeing you, I saw you again
your brown eyes crossed mine, but you didn't smile, nor
did you stare
it wasn't like usual
you looked away as fast as you could
I wanted to come up to you
to talk to you, like the good old times
I wanted to hear your voice, hear you saying my name
only you could make it sound so beautiful

I wanted to tell you how much I miss you,
how much I love you
but I didn't

I was afraid
what if you reject me?
it would break me all over again
it would bring back all the pain

I was afraid
what if there was another chance?
we would fall in love with each other all over again
everything would be perfect

I was stubborn
so were you
both of us decided to not say a word to each other
and I guess
we'll never know
we'll be stuck forever with the two ugly words
what if

the voices in my head are getting too loud
making everything harder for me
lying to me that I won't get better
but between all those voices making me sick,
I hear yours
telling me everything's alright
and it will be fine
that I will get through this
and will be happy
that I will find my happiness too
and the reason for that won't be you

I see you're with her now
it hurts, I admit
the one I used to call mine
is now kissing her lips

I should've told you
I love you
I should've let you know
there is another chance
for us to start something new
something different

I should've given you the chance
to be better
to make up for your mistakes
I should've told you
I love you
I should've made sure
you knew you could come back

I should've told you
I miss you

I hate how I wake up and you disappear

one day I'll replace you just like you replaced me

I broke my own heart by waiting for you
thinking you would come back
hoping our love story didn't end
I don't even know why I keep blaming you
when all you did was leave me with the truth
while I made up a lie

messages I wanted to send you
wanted to call you so many times but didn't
my heart was crying for you, it needed you here
so many things I wanted to tell you but never had the
chance to

do you still remember me or does she make you forget
my name?

in my dreams – mine
in reality – hers

honestly I don't know where it went wrong
honey, what did I do to lose you?

I really wish I said something back then,
anything, just to keep you here

as I look in the mirror I see that I'm still wearing the
necklace
the one you gave me for our anniversary
a year ago
and I still can't take it off
cause whenever I touch it
the memories rush through my head
I feel you putting it on me
and telling me I look good with your initial around my
neck
once again I touch it
trying to take it off
I hear your voice telling me not to
don't give up on me
wait a little bit more and I promise you
I'll be back

remember me as the girl who made you happy
the one who made sure that when you went through
hell it felt like heaven just because of me

holding your hand during those hard times
never letting you go
and fighting your demons with you

remember me as the girl who loved you
even though sometimes it felt like you didn't deserve it

my heart is hurting
and you're not here to fix it

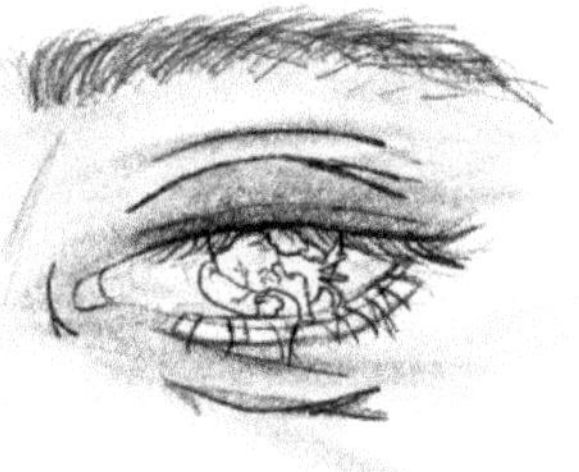
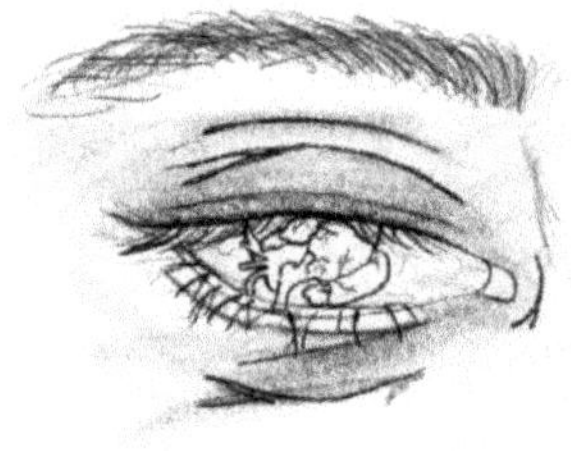

I miss being loved
being loved by you

I miss being held
by those hands of yours

your voice
comforting me and telling me everything will be fine

your eyes
staring right into mine

I miss loving you
I miss you loving me

one day I'll find my happiness too
with or without you

you found a girl deserving of your love
someone who will never hurt you
a girl you could trust
the one who you can give your heart to
someone who will never break it
who'll give you more than you'll ever give her
more than what you deserve

love
hope
trust
respect
loyalty

a girl you got bored of so quickly
so easily
and left her in the same way
your ex left you
just for her to move on to someone
and repeat
repeat the damage you've done to her
to someone else

you found a girl
a girl with a golden heart
you found me

I never left you
you pushed me away

if I die today
I want everyone
including you
to know
that I never ever
not even for a second
stopped loving you

wish I could go back to the time
when everything between us was just fine

I guess forgetting you is impossible after all
especially when I'm alone at night
or when I need someone to talk to
someone who would listen to my crying heart
someone who would fix it
someone who would fix *me*
someone like you

my heart belongs to someone who doesn't want it
it belongs to you my love

I look up and see your eyes
your smile makes my heart beat faster
legs are shaking as I run to you
but the moment I put my arms around you
you disappear

losing my mind trying to understand yours

I see it now
she's prettier and smarter
nicer and softer
she doesn't fight with you, she tries to solve the
problems between you two
she is everything you've ever wanted
she is not me, she's better

I knew you were going to leave
when you started acting different
your eyes didn't light up anymore
and that's when I knew
there wasn't an us anymore

I only fall asleep when I think about you
knowing you'll visit me in my dreams

2 a.m. with you on my mind

I'd forgive you the minute you ask me to
I'd take you back without hesitation
I'd leave all the mistakes in the past
to start a new chapter with you

I tried everything to keep you but you still left

am I wasting my time by waiting for you without you
telling me to?

I thought you were *playing* her
just like you did the others
and then when it gets boring
you'd come back
but the truth is - you didn't
and what hurts more is that you never even left her

you
told me to leave but never let
me

I keep daydreaming about you and your love
I feel your ghost next to me
telling me that your body just doesn't want to listen to
your soul wanting me
I have the version of you that I love here
so what else do I need
except for your touch
and a real image of you

miss your laugh

I want summer back
I want your love back
I want you back

don't worry,
I'll write the happy ending we deserved
and I'll live in that lie
which will keep me alive

I don't know why I still miss you
I don't know why I still blame myself for everything
you've done

I remember seeing you for the first time
your eyes were the first thing I noticed
I was locked in them
they were the reason I liked you in the first place
then I got to know you
you told me about your past and opened up to me
that was when I fell in love with you
but your eyes, oh honey
art

oh honey
hell feels like heaven with you

when the sun comes up
and the flowers start to bloom
promise me you'll come back soon

when the moon shows up
and the wolves start to cry
assure me our love isn't a lie

another day passes by
without you seeing my smile
and when I look up to the sky
I see the stars shining bright

the day comes to an end
and my lover still hasn't returned

I can't imagine myself with someone else
I don't want anyone else but you
please
stay

take my hand and never leave me alone
hold me close and don't you ever let me go
put your arms around me, don't let me slip away
whisper in my ear I'm the one you want

I kissed him
all I could taste were cigarettes and the liquor he had
been drinking
I knew
just like his nicotine addiction wasn't good for him
he wasn't good for me

late night
full moon
shining stars
lying here
all alone
begging God
to bring you home
asking Him to fill your heart with love
keep you safe
keep you warm

my soul left my body the moment you left me

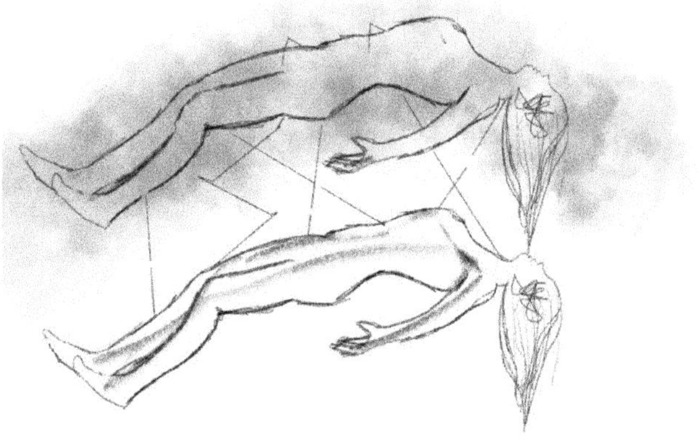

he tells me he loves me
and wants me to be his again
to be with him forever
and never ever leave his side

he tells me he loves me
and wants to marry me
that he will fly to the moon with me
and never come back

he tells me he loves me
and regrets leaving me
that he wants a second chance

he tells me he hates me
the liquor has left his system
all the nice words have become harsh harassments

the door closed
and a heart was broken

when you're out there with her
I'm lying in our bed waiting for your call

the sun comes up
and I know it's time for us to say goodbye
when you sneak out on me
and leave your love behind
7 o'clock
the time is ticking
taking my lover away from me
knowing that this is the last time I see you
the last time I can call you mine, I hug you tighter
one last time
let me tell you that I love you
one last time
let me feel your love
"it's almost 8", you say
"I have to leave. This is the last time, my love, I'm not coming back. Wear warm clothes and make sure to sleep and eat well. I won't be here to look out for you anymore. You're by yourself now, know that I still love you, but this has to end. This was the last time, goodbye."

during this hour
you're the only one I miss
oh honey, it was an honor
to have gotten your kiss

my favorite part of the day is
when I close my eyes
and feel your arms around me

it looks like you found your true love and it's not me

the moon isn't ours anymore
and you don't love me no more

I know I should move on,
keep you in the past
but honey we still have so much to do
and I'm not ready to let go of you

another morning without you
trying my best to not call you

I thought you were afraid of losing me
I thought you wouldn't survive it
thought it would be your death
guess she saved you

writing about you is the only thing that's keeping me
alive
it gives me a feeling that you're not gone
like you're still here
I know it's crazy and unhealthy
but it's the only thing keeping me here
you're saving me from myself

the scars you left are killing me
the love I still have for you – saving me

tell me honey, am I a fool for still loving you?

they say it's hard to forget someone you loved
I can prove them wrong by using you
the one who forgot me

lately, I've been thinking about you
what you're doing and if you're fine
lately, I've kept myself so busy with you
I forgot to look after myself

you can't just come back whenever you feel like it
and bring your negativity back into my life

you can't leave when I'm getting used to you
and leave me broken again

you can't just use me when she isn't there
and disappear when she comes back

you can't take advantage of my love like that
I promise you
I promise myself
this was the last time

lately, I suck at writing
trying to describe what I feel for you
lately, I've been trying to lose the feelings I have for you
lately, I've been missing you
even though you were never really mine

what is it about you that makes me fall in love with you
more and more everyday instead of forgetting you?

baby you're my drug
I won't lie
I can't get enough

you told me you love me but it felt like you didn't mean
it
your hug didn't feel warm anymore
and my name - beautiful

I love how you visit me in my dreams and tell me all the
things I want to hear

I wish I loved myself as much as I love you
I wish I could accept and love my flaws
I wish I could ignore what others say about me like I
ignore their comments about you
I wish I could look in the mirror and adore the person
standing there
I wish I could love the person that loves you
I wish I could love myself

you've changed since you left
the way you act
dress and talk
you became a better version of yourself
and this, all for her

it's not my fault you couldn't keep your promise
it's not my fault that you left

the moon is helping me to forget you
listening to my problems
and wiping away my tears

I love reading everything I wrote about you
it's the only way to keep the memory of you

maybe if we met in another lifetime
or if the world was kinder to us
the sky bluer
and the sun brighter
maybe I could've been yours
maybe you could've been mine

I'd make you happy if you'd let me

you found your way into my soul
nice words and a sweet smile
got out of there the minute you got in
leaving harsh words and pain

Lamara Djabraïlova

even if it's not real
I can feel you here with me
and whenever you fade away
I take another shot
to make sure you'll stay

you keep writing about her
and so do I
the difference is
one of us loves her
while the other despises her

I'd take you back if you'd come back
without asking you why you left

I'd pick up the phone if you call
I never deleted your number
just in case, maybe I'll need it someday

I'd come to your place if you ask me to
even if it'd be late at night
just to comfort you and give you the feeling that you're
not alone

I'd die for you
take a bullet that was meant for you

I'd do everything to keep you happy
without asking for anything in return

you think I've moved on
because I didn't contact you for so long
but baby the truth is
your ghost is here
telling me all the things I want to hear
keeping me company
keeping me alive

Lamara Djabraïlova

I love looking at the moon and thinking about you

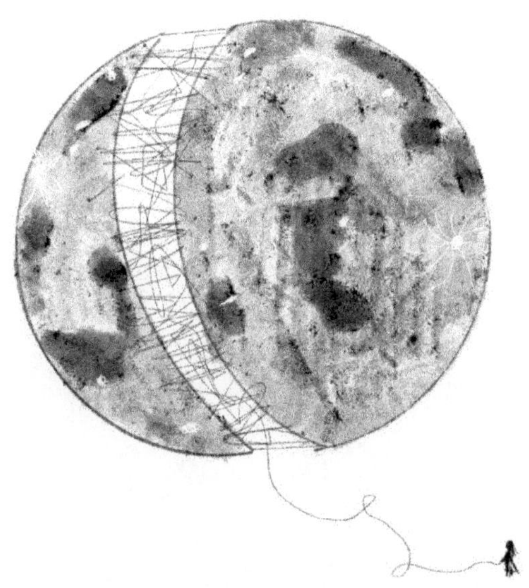

may our eyes meet again
and our hands finally touch
may I hear your voice calling for me
and feel your love
may I see you again
and repeat the words you once told me
my love for you will never die
my love for you will never die

and now she has you
half of me
my soulmate
unfortunately I wasn't yours
never was

not writing about you will make me forget you
a few more pages to go
and I promise I'll let you go

losing myself in my thoughts
losing myself trying to remember you

the tears won't stop falling down
my heart is still crying for you
my soul looking for yours

a reminder:
you deserve more than what he gives you
you deserve better
take your stuff and leave
because he won't
he won't leave the girl that loves him
cares about him
feeds him
gives him all he needs
he will not leave you
not because he loves you
but because you love him
you love him enough for him to want you to stay
he wants your love
not you

I finally realized
I was in love with the love I gave you
not realizing that
just me loving you wasn't enough
all this time
I was the one who deserved my own love
first me
and only then - you

I want you more than I ever wanted me

every time I close my eyes you're here
so maybe if I don't open them ever again
I'll finally be with my man

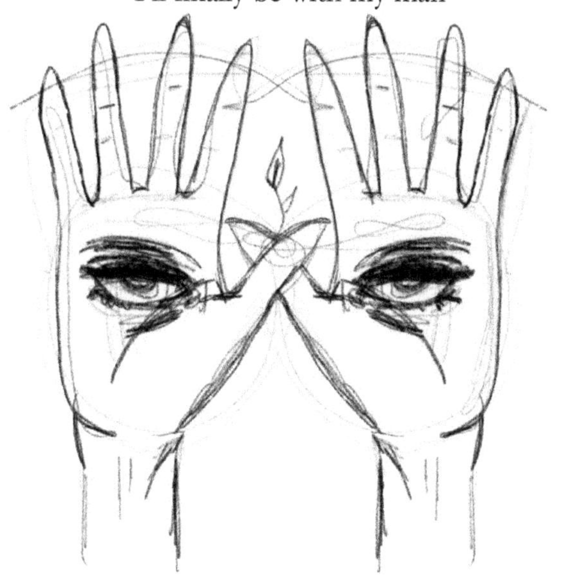

I always tell you how I miss you at night
but let me tell you about the day, my love
the house is so empty without you
the bed so cold

you're the first one I think about when I wake up
and the last when I go to sleep
the room misses your laughter, just like I do actually
it's been weeks since the couch has felt your warmth
my neck – your breathing

it's freezing in here, my love
I need you home

I wish I could make a wish
a real one
one that will come true
I wish I could make a wish
and wish for you

he's a writer
just like me
he writes about love
confessing it to the one he loves

just like me, he goes to sleep with those thoughts
and when I think about him
the one I love
his thoughts are with her
the one he desires

I desire for a love like mine
being loved by someone
the same way I love

I have these dreams where I see you
everything is perfect and it looks so real
but when I wake up, it doesn't feel like waking up at all
you still hold my hand and beg me not to leave
"I want you to stay", you tell me, "don't open your eyes,
please"
then within a second everything turns black and I can't
see a thing
I try to move but I can't
I feel your touch and try to open my eyes
"I'm still here," I hear your voice, "just don't open your
eyes, please stay with me"
"This is just a dream," I answer, "this is not real, you
left me months ago"
suddenly I can move my hand and there you are
I look up to you and see you smiling
"See, I told you. I'm still here, I never left you, my love.
I will never leave you, I love you, I promise"
"I've never heard you telling me this, this was the first
time you confessed to me" I smile
the door opens and once again you disappear, "Honey,
who are you talking to?"

My last words to you

as I'm writing down the words you told me
and the promises you made me
I realize
it's time to choose myself now

loving you > loving myself

loving you was easy for me
all my attention and appreciation would go to you
loving you kind of kept me busy
that way I wouldn't have any time for myself
but now you're gone and I don't have anyone to give it
to
I have no option but to give it to myself
I have to look at myself in the mirror
forced to love my flaws
and it's scaring me
and every time I tried to escape it
I'd look for someone else to love
and every time it would work and I'd forget about
myself
but now when there's no one around but me
I have to give myself the love I used to give to you
it's something new and feels like a waste of my love
loving myself doesn't seem right
it's like I don't deserve it
I feel like I have to change the way I look and talk
I feel like I don't deserve my own love
someone like me doesn't deserve my own love

Lamara Djabraïlova

also by Lamara Djabrailova

Daniël en Nora
because, about and for you

Contact us on Instagram!
Author: @lamaradjabrailova
Illustrator: @emmartful
Editor: @e__ditto

Milton Keynes UK
Ingram Content Group UK Ltd.
UKHW011959011223
433643UK00001B/65